SPIRITUAL
HOUSE
CLEANING

Tom Donnan

SPIRITUAL
HOUSE
CLEANING

Tom Donnan

Gazelle
PRESS

Mobile, Alabama

Spiritual Housecleaning
by Tom Donnan
Copyright ©2015 Tom Donnan

Unless otherwise identified, Scripture is taken from the Holy Bible, New International Version. Copyright ©1973, 1978, 1984 by International Bible Society. Used by permission of International Bible Society.

ISBN 978-1-58169-578-6
For Worldwide Distribution
Printed in the U.S.A.
Gazelle Press
P.O. Box 191540 • Mobile, AL 36619
800-367-8203

Table of Contents

Acknowledgments

I want to thank my children for their unfailing love and support. I love being their dad and ever going before them in life. Let me tell you again, raising you kids were the best years of my life. We have had fun! I love you very much.

I have a wonderful friendship with Pastor Phillip Corbett and his wife. Phil has opened many wonderful doors for me. In the times I have traveled with him, I would speak before the main service. In those times as I have used the prayers in this booklet I have seen God touch the lives of His children. I am very grateful Phil has been mentoring me.

I want to thank Need Him Ministries. In their chat forum I have been able to pray with people around the world. What a privilege to see God touch the lives of His children, here in the USA and many other countries! It has been an honor each and every time I can help a person receive Jesus and they become born again.

I would like to thank the Banashak family (Gazelle Press) for taking me on as a new author. Since the economic downturn of 2007, no publishing companies were taking on new writers. This publishing family has blessed me. Through the first book and now this one, we will be reaching many people for Jesus. Thank you very much.

Introduction

In this journey Father God has brought me down many interesting paths. In the valley times, the Holy Spirit has led me to develop unique prayers for my life and family. Now He is directing me to share the prayers in print form.

From the very beginning of my walk with Him, the Lord has allowed me to step into the supernatural. When I was just a babe in the faith, I had an experience I couldn't explain. I met Jesus! He was in the clouds; His clothes were whiter than white, and His eyes could see everything about me. As I approached Him just a few feet away, I dropped to my knees and sobbed. My heart was breaking. I had one issue on my heart and mind—I deeply knew that while I lived my life, I could have done more for Jesus and now I had intense regrets. Instantly I woke up in my room. This was very real. I was forever changed and now I strive to work for Jesus.

In 2006 I had a heart attack and died. In a nano second I was in the spiritual realm when God spoke to me. He said, "It is only while you are on Earth that you can work for Jesus." Then bam! They hit me with the paddles to restart my heart. Three days later while I was still in intensive care, a doctor asked me: "How does it feel to be back from the dead?"

Looking into the face of my own mortality brought about some thoughts. *What actions in my life will last for Jesus? What will make it through the fire and will not be burned up and of no spiritual gain at the end of my life the next time I die?* So I prayed that God would use me. Being an intercessor brings me joy. When God shows up and brings change to another person's life as a result of my prayers, it's very satisfying. Let's see what God may have for you to do after you read this book.

I have deliberately arranged this book so that the prayers bring about different steps with spiritual applications. First and foremost, a person must be saved so that is where we begin. All the other prayers will work off this position. By the last prayer, it is my hope your life and home have been spiritually cleansed and ready for God's visitations.

These are the days of Joel 2:28, the outpouring of His Holy Spirit.

> *And afterward, I will pour out my Spirit on all people. Your sons and daughters will prophesy, your old men will dream dreams, your young men will see visions.*

As He touches your life through these prayers, let God receive all the glory! Get ready and expect Him to do great things!

1

Salvation

I get funny looks from people when I bring up the subject of spiritual housecleaning. It is a foreign concept for many today to use spiritual tools to set our lives and homes aside for God. However, as the darkness increases in our day, we are more in need of the presence of God in our home sanctuaries than ever before.

How can evil invade our homes if we belong to Christ? This is a common question I hear from believers. It has to do with spiritual doors. Each member of a family can open a spiritual door to good or to evil that will affect the entire group. As I learned about this subject, the Lord allowed me to endure spiritual challenges until I received a breakthrough and grasped the tools and keys He wanted me to have. They were interesting lessons but not fun.

Today I look at those experiences as learning how

to be a trailblazer for the Christian community. Why? As never before Americans are throwing open the doors to occult activities and, as a result, darkness is increasing. I believe we are going to see levels of evil we have not yet experienced. Isn't it just like God to prepare a people for just the right time and hour?

We need to remember that in Exodus 20, God says He is a jealous God. This means if we have material and items in our homes that are connected with other gods, it offends Him. We need to be on a quest to eliminate all things in our homes and hearts that He would find offensive. The desired result is to have His wonderful presence in our homes.

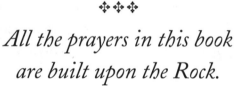

All the prayers in this book are built upon the Rock.

Two weeks ago I was connected with a pastor in Malawi, Africa. I sent him two books, but it would be at least two weeks before they arrived. So I emailed him the anointing technique and prayers I have included in these pages to be used on his church and home.

That night, after anointing his home, they had a small group prayer meeting. God showed up in a thick atmosphere and everyone there was immersed in it. He told me how wonderful the night was and how all his family were blessed. This is what I am hoping will happen in your home for your family!

All the prayers in this book are built upon the Rock. Jesus said, "And I tell you that you are Peter, and on this rock I will build my church, and the gates of Hades will not overcome it" (Matthew 16:18). *Matthew Henry's Commentary* on this Scripture offers the following explanation:

> The word translated "rock" is not the same word as "Peter," but is of a similar meaning. Nothing can be more wrong than to suppose that Christ meant the person of Peter was the rock. Without doubt Christ Himself is the Rock, the tried foundation of the church; and woe to him that attempts to lay any other!

In Exodus 20:1-3, Moses begins to receive the Ten Commandments:

> *And God spoke all these words: "I am the Lord your God, who brought you out of Egypt, out of the land of slavery. You shall have no other gods before me."*

When God is our first love,
we are in a position to receive
the best of His blessings!

The point of this passage is that God must have first place in a Christian's heart. Jesus must be the center of our lives. When God is our first love, we are in position to receive the best of His blessings!

Sin is the pivotal issue in our relationship with God. We are born into this life; it is a gift. While we are here on Earth, we must find a way to have a relationship with Him. Deuteronomy 4:29 says,

> *But if from there you seek the Lord your God, you will find him if you seek him with all your heart and with all your soul.*

When we seek to know Him, He will always bring us to His Son, Jesus, because He is the way and the truth and the life (John 14:6). When we accept Christ's finished work on the cross, the shedding of His blood for all sins, we are saved.

Father God is holy; man is not. Our heavenly

Father required one human being, Jesus, to live a sinless life. Jesus also freely chose to give up that life to pay the price for everyone's sins. For this precise reason, He came into the world.

We all need to ask ourselves some basic, questions about the Christian faith. Some questions to ponder are:

- Do you believe there is only one triune God—the Father, the Son, and the Holy Spirit?

- Do you believe that Jesus Christ is the Son of God?

- Do you believe Jesus was born of a virgin?

- Do you believe Jesus lived a sinless life?

- Do you believe Jesus was fully man and fully God?

- Do you believe Jesus Christ shed His blood on the cross to pay the price God required for all sins?

- Do you believe Jesus Christ died and rose again?

- Are you willing to relinquish control of your life and follow Him?

- Are you willing to confess your sins and leave that life behind?

If you have answered yes to all these questions, let's pray together to receive Jesus as Savior and Lord. If you have already prayed the sinner's prayer, you can pray the following prayer to recommit yourself to Jesus.

Dear Father God,

I thank You for Your Son, Jesus, and the work He did on the cross. I know He willingly shed His blood to pay the price for all mankind's sins. I confess to You, Father, that I am a sinner. I am sorry for the pain my sins have caused You; please forgive me. Now I invite You, Jesus, to come into my heart and into my life. I want to live for You. In Jesus' name, amen.

If you have prayed this prayer for the first time, you are a new creation in Christ Jesus! Being a new creation in Christ simply means that the Holy Spirit has now entered your spirit, you are now in God's family, and you now have eternal life with Him. Your name has been written in the Lamb's Book of Life.

You see, when God looks upon you, He sees His Son, Jesus. Trusting Jesus is the only way to the kingdom of heaven—not through any good works we might do or have done. Salvation is Jesus in us.

So what should happen next? What I call "spiritual housecleaning" is now in order. As you will see, by closing spiritual doors to evil, we can open windows and doors to God and His blessings.

2

Spiritual Housecleaning

What is spiritual housecleaning and why would you want to do it? This line of thought was born out of my own personal need. I was experiencing some spiritual problems in my life, and I did not understand how being a child of God affected my life and home. After all, didn't being saved, born again, and washed in the blood automatically mean evil couldn't harm me? I found the answer to that question is a resounding NO!

I have an inquisitive prayer life. I want to understand and comprehend matters. I want to know how the spiritual realm operates and how good and evil work in our physical world. Even though I want answers, I'm a slow learner. It takes me a lot of time even to formulate a meaningful question about my situation.

One day as I was pondering my plight, the question of questions came to me. I asked God, "How is evil entering my life and house?"

✛ ✛ ✛

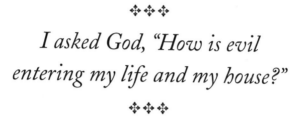

I asked God, "How is evil entering my life and my house?"

✛ ✛ ✛

He gave me the simplest answer. "Through spiritual doors."

For instance, when did sin enter the lives of Adam and Eve? The Bible says it happened when they were tempted and then ate the forbidden fruit from the tree of knowledge of good and evil.

The Fall

Now the serpent was more crafty than any of the wild animals the Lord God had made. He said to the woman, "Did God really say, 'You must not eat from any tree in the garden'?"

The woman said to the serpent, "We may eat fruit from the trees in the garden, but God did say, 'You must not eat fruit from the tree that is in the middle of the garden, and you must not touch it, or you will die.'"

"You will not certainly die," the serpent said to the woman. "For God knows that when you eat from it your eyes will be opened, and you will be like God, knowing good and evil."

When the woman saw that the fruit of the tree was good for food and pleasing to the eye, and also desirable for gaining wisdom, she took some and ate it. She also gave some to her husband, who was with her, and he ate it. Then the eyes of both of them were opened, and they realized they were naked; so they sewed fig leaves together and made coverings for themselves (Genesis 3:1-7)

The choices we make can swing open the door to either godliness and blessings or to evil influences."

When a thought entered their mind, a choice flowed out of their hearts. The spiritual realm encapsulates our emotional heart and mind. The choices we make can swing open the door to either godliness and blessings or to evil influences and the consequences of sin. These verses of Scripture illustrate the fall of mankind and the eternal struggle every person must face as a result.

We are generational people with a family blood-line. We receive our family heritage, the legacy passed from one generation to the next, at birth. Those who went before us contribute to the spiritual atmosphere of our lives. The book of Exodus shows us this connection.

The Ten Commandments

And God spoke all these words: "I am the Lord your God, who brought you out of Egypt, out of the land of slavery. You shall have no other gods before me. You shall not make for yourself an image in the form of anything in heaven above or on the earth beneath or in the waters below. You shall not bow down to them or worship them; for I, the Lord your God, am a jealous God, punishing the children for the sin of the parents to the third and fourth generation of those who hate me, but showing love to a thousand generations of those who love me and keep my commandments" (Exodus 20:1-6).

First, let me establish that when a person becomes a born-again believer, he enters into a covenant relationship with his heavenly Father. He is agreeing to live by God's guidelines. However, when a Christian chooses to sin, he steps outside those guidelines, and the effects of wrong choices begin.

I believe the most serious violation of our agreement to live by God's guidelines is taking Him out of first place in our hearts and placing something else in that top position. This is the beginning of forsaking Him.

When a Christian chooses to sin,
he steps outside those guidelines,
and the effects
of wrong choices begin.

To further understand the effects this choice can have, read Deuteronomy 28, the blessings or curses chapter. I believe all Christians want the blessings and hope contained within this chapter and pray that the curses or consequences will not be a part of their lives. The pivotal verse in Deuteronomy is 28:20,

The Lord will send on you curses, confusion and rebuke in everything you put your hand to, until you are destroyed and come to sudden ruin because of the evil you have done in forsaking him.

I frequently meet people who say, "That's the Old Testament, and it no longer applies in our day." First Corinthians 10 says otherwise. In verse 11, Paul is talking about Israel's history and says,

These things happened to them as examples and were written down as warnings for us, on whom the culmination of the ages has come.

The Apostle Paul doesn't discount these truths. Rather, he carefully builds a bridge to the them.

According to Deuteronomy 28:1-14, God blesses those who hold Him as their first love and give Him the most important place in their heart. Exodus 20:6

God blesses those who hold Him as their first love and give Him the most important place in their heart.

says that if God stays in the first place of every believer's heart, His blessings will flow for a thousand generations. To be sure, all humans long to have His blessings in their lives and family line.

Do not fail to note that God also says He will punish the sins of the parents upon the children—to the third and fourth generation. Following those first fourteen verses of blessing in Deuteronomy 28 are fifty-three verses laying out the curses that we fall under if we are not obedient to Him. And Jeremiah 32:18 says,

You show love to thousands but bring the punish-ment for the parents' sins into the laps of their children after them.

What I see at play in these passages are the dynamics of legal grounds—grasping why and how evil is permitted to affect a person's life. Legal grounds are "the lasting effects of sin." They are sins that have not been repented of, so they're not forgiven.

But you might say, "I was washed in the blood of the Lamb. Wasn't every sin forgiven when I trusted Christ?" Yes, in becoming new creations in Christ Jesus, our souls are washed in the blood, but the legal grounds are not automatically released.

I love the song "I Surrender All." It tells us that our walk with Christ is an ongoing process of submitting our will to His. We must constantly yield and surrender to Him the portions of our mind and heart that hold open doorways to evil's attacks.

We must constantly yield and surrender to Him the portions of our mind and heart that hold open doorways to evil's attacks.

I learned these truths when the Lord started me on a spiritual journey to gain understanding of my family's generational sin. As I walked on this path, God began to expose the sins in my father's family line. The Lord revealed more family information to me in six weeks than other family members had learned in ten years. For example, once I was following a librarian to find a book, and I caught a mere glimpse of a book out of alignment with all the other books on the shelf. I grabbed the book as I passed. When I opened it, I found pertinent family information inside that book.

When I was visiting my sister in Phoenix, Arizona, we stopped by a local book store. As we headed toward the section she desired to visit, I leaned down and picked up a book lying flat on a counter. Again I found family information within its pages. God was showing me the sins rooted in my family bloodline.

Because we prayed corporately,
the sins were forgiven,
the legal grounds were cancelled,
and those spiritual doors
were closed.

At the end of this spiritual journey, I got together with Christian family members, and we prayed for those sins to be forgiven. Because we prayed corporately, the sins were forgiven, the legal grounds were cancelled, and those spiritual doors were closed. God ended the cycle of the sins of the parents being visited upon the children. My Christian relatives and I stood together in the gap for our family bloodline, thereby ending the effects of our forefathers' sin from my father's side of the family upon our lives.

When this cycle ended and after I'd had a rest from this particular search, God again called me to journey—this time down the path of my mother's family bloodline. Just as with my father's side of the family, I learned of my mother's family secrets and sins. Whereas my father's family had come from Northern Ireland and Scotland, my mother's side of the family emigrated from Germany. I found that the generational issues were different, but all the same, the sins of the fathers needed to be addressed.

I don't want to be confusing as I address these generational sins. I have used the words "parents" and "forefathers" somewhat interchangeably, since forefather simply means a member of the past generations of your family. It was our forefathers' sins that opened a door through their hearts and, as a result, evil entered the family.

I realized I needed to build a foundational prayer to end my family's generational sins. I didn't understand at the time that the Lord would use me as an intercessor for others too. He gave me a mandate found in Isaiah 57:13b-14, which says:

> *"But whoever takes refuge in me will inherit the land and possess my holy mountain." And it will be said: "Build up, build up, prepare the road! Remove the obstacles out of the way of my people."*

He now wanted me to apply the knowledge I had gained in my lessons to His children. Allow me to share the following prayer that God led me to pray with my relatives. You can also pray this prayer for your family's generational sins.

Dear Father God,

I lift Your children up to You. Please cover them with the blood of Jesus Christ from the top of their heads to the bottoms of their feet. Lord, assign protecting angels, ministering angels, and a high-ranking angel to Your children. Also, please forgive their forefathers for the sins they have committed that have caused You pain. We are sorry for the pain it has caused You. Please forgive them.

Lord, please forgive the forefathers who have forsaken You for other gods. Though they once knew You, they placed another god in Your place. We are sorry for the pain their forsaking of You has caused You. Please forgive them now.

Heavenly Father, in the name of Jesus, we break off every curse, stronghold, and grounds from their lives and set them free. In Jesus' name, amen.

If you have prayed this prayer from your heart, the generational sins that have plagued your family have come to an end. You will begin to see changes. The old spiritual legacy is over, and the blessings are about to begin.

3

Personal Sin

I love to talk to people who have recently been born again. Their spirits are light, and they walk in a new freedom of life. According to 2 Corinthians 5:17, that person has become a new creation in Christ Jesus:

Therefore, if anyone is in Christ, the new creation has come; the old has gone, the new is here!

Born-again people have been washed in the blood of the Lamb. The Holy Spirit enters their spirit, and a new walk of life begins. The Holy Spirit now empowers them to overcome sin. The person who is newly filled with the love of God will find that all things are now new, and life feels good.

In my new beginning, a time came when healing from my past needed to happen. At this time I had just suffered my first heart attack. I call myself a "stuffer." I stuffed my emotional hurts, pain, and trauma deep inside my spirit and hid them in my mind. I was stuffed all right, but I failed to notice that the effects of "stuffing" were literally gushing out all over the place. The truth is, I was still living in denial. However, the heart attack woke me up to a new need in my life—the need to surrender the secret places in my mind.

In that secret place, I had hung a veil over the doorway of a room and added a warning sign: "Do not enter!" I had even forgotten some things I had hidden in there. But God knew that the hurts and pain I had secretly tucked away gave grounds to evil. They allowed evil to access my life and limit the healing flow of God.

When we are walking in our new life with Jesus, we have to understand that we will be hurt by other people, causing us to need to grow in Christlikeness and to move into emotional and spiritual healthiness. This growth has been a process for me and has taken time. As I read the Scriptures, I allowed the truth of God's Word to renew my mind. In order to lay the proper groundwork for the truth God wants me to share, I must confess that even after thirty-one years of following Jesus, I have encountered some difficult times in my life. As a result of those difficulties, I've sometimes lacked forgiveness in my heart.

For example, in a year's time, I was living day by

day with serious relationship problems, my sister died of congestive heart failure, and my job was spiraling downward. With all three crisis situations running together, I was living in survival mode. I lived one day

*I needed to invite God
to search my heart in order
to keep me on track.*

at a time, stuffing my feelings and emotions inside and hoping I could work out the issues later. I felt like a water balloon with a phobia of pins. I was ready to burst. I was laid off after forty-two years with the same company. A month later, my sister passed, and my relationship problems continued. Toward the end of this cycle, I learned a valuable lesson found in Psalm 139:23-24:

> *Search me, God, and know my heart; test me and know my anxious thoughts. See if there is any offensive way in me, and lead me in the way everlasting.*

I needed to invite God to search my heart in order to keep me on track. Unknowingly, I had opened doors to evil's attacks by not asking for my heavenly Father's help in seeing the statutes of my darkened heart.

Please read Psalm 139. I find this passage comforting since it helps me to see that God knows each one of us intimately. Allowing God access into the secret places in our heart and mind helps us to be pure in heart, spotless, and holy before Him.

I want my life to bring change for the kingdom of God. I have read biographies and autobiographies about men and women of God who walked so closely with the Holy Spirit that He could minister with them and through them. God's servant and the Holy Spirit worked together in a tangible way.

When I pray with people and God shows up to touch their lives, healing and freedom come. I strive to minister to others and bring eternal benefits to them. May I encourage you to take time often to ask God to search your heart for any pain or sins hidden in the secret place of your heart? When God brings a hidden issue to your mind, please deal with it swiftly and biblically. Keep your spiritual clothing pure and white before the Lord. Learn to be quick to forgive and slow to be offended.

Let's pray the following together:

Dear Father,

Search my heart and reveal to me any unforgiveness I have toward others. Please release Your grace for me to forgive anyone who has hurt me. Lord, show me where I have stepped into personal sins and empower me to turn from them. Give me strength to overcome temptations and be true to Your ways. I give You authority to come into all areas in my life, and I surrender all of myself to You. In Jesus' name, amen.

4

Cords and Soul Ties

God has made our hearts to be connected to others. Throughout life, relationships are forged and bonds are made. I call these connections cords and soul ties. Godly ties are beneficial to every Christian's life. People who love us and contribute to our wellbeing bring us joy.

On the other hand, ungodly ties bring difficulties, heartache, and pain, and these ties will hinder our relationship with God. Cords can be forged through abuse and trauma as well as through our own choices. When we seek to love God with our whole heart, mind, and soul, He has compassion upon us and longs to bless our lives and bring us into new freedom.

The subject of cords and soul ties can be and often is controversial. At times, we entertain a thought, a feeling, or a compulsion to sin, and we simply don't know where those inclinations come from. Consequently, we may think we are bad or sinful, and those thoughts are a part of our personality. However, I have learned from my own experience that when I break the cords to an unhealthy situation, my life gets better. The thoughts, feelings, or compulsions that I had within me were really coming from some of the ties I had developed with others.

By faith I saw God close some additional spiritual doors for me, and life became even better!

When I was new in my faith, I began listening to a call-in radio program on this particular subject. When the number was given to call in with questions, I dialed it. I still feel that day was one of those God times. My call quickly went through the switchboard. When I asked my question, the pastor confirmed my notion of cords and encouraged me to pray for God to break those that involved unhealthy relationships. I did and felt instant relief. By faith, I saw God close some additional spiritual doors for me, and life became even better!

The following is the prayer I use when helping others to be freed from their cords and soul ties:

Dear Father,

I lift up before You (your name). Please gather together into a bundle any ungodly soul ties or any traumatic events that forge cords to other people. In the name of Jesus, we now cut those cords and separate (name) from those ungodly soul ties and cords, and we ask that You make (name's) spirit whole and of one piece where no evil thoughts can penetrate. In Jesus' name, amen.

5

For Your Home

When people are looking to buy a home, most of them will buy one that's already built. Others will choose to have a new home built on a piece of land.

Most people don't know the history behind a home, an apartment building, a condominium, or any other piece of real estate. Because I am spiritually sensitive, I have learned the need for cleansing my home or the place where I will be sleeping. Sins do take place in our homes and in other buildings. Sins have also taken place upon the land where a dwelling has been built. For that reason, it is important to pray for the forgiveness of those sins and to cover our homes in the blood of Jesus. I am a firm believer in the need to anoint our homes and set them aside for God's presence to be with us.

I learned this important lesson out of need. I was experiencing spiritual trouble in my home. It got so bad that I knew I needed to seek definite answers. In my search, I was led to people who taught me about anointing my home.

I am a firm believer in the need to anoint our homes and set them aside for God's presence to be with us.

Anointing a home is much like the anointing of the tent of the meeting in Exodus 40:9. The oil represents the Holy Spirit. By anointing with oil, you are spiritually setting aside the structure and the land for God.

Anointing oil can be purchased at any local Christian bookstore or in a pinch, you can use simple cooking oil that is stocked in your kitchen. Pray for the Holy Spirit to be with the anointing as you walk throughout the dwelling, symbolically touching the windows and doorways or any other entry points to the spiritual realm. Then pray throughout the house and ask God to wash it clean. My usual practice is even to include going to the property lines and releasing oil upon the ground.

In a church I was attending several years ago, an elder asked me if I would come to his sister's home to pray. As I tell this story, I will warn you that it is dramatic and on the far end of the scale, but it illustrates my point about anointing one's dwelling. If we have not anointed our home and prayed over it, it has not been spiritually cleansed. No one had anointed or prayed over this home.

If we have not anointed our home and prayed over it, it has not been spiritually cleansed.

The following is her story. This lady was having spiritual problems in her home. Her babysitter even told the lady that if she did not correct the problem, she would no longer go into her house to babysit. I learned that she had been a missionary nurse in Cameroon, Africa, for ten years. While she was serving there, she came home one day to find a tribal witchdoctor's spell hanging on the front doorknob of her home. She removed it and cleaned up the door. However, an evil spirit had entered her life.

Fast forward to her return trip home in the States.

She had now unknowingly brought that spiritual element into her home, causing even more discomfort. The television set would unexplainably turn off and on. A ball of light could be seen in different rooms. Obviously, these occurrences were frightening to this family.

This former missionary nurse's two brothers and I formed a prayer team with her. We began by praying over each person's life. Then we went from room to room, anointing the windows and doorway frames. We dabbed our finger in the blessed oil and then touched the doorways and windows—each a symbolic entry point to the spiritual realm. If we felt any particular item in a room needed to be anointed, we did so. Many artifacts she had collected in Africa hung on her walls as decorations. They were memories of her time of serving the Lord overseas, and we anointed many of them.

As we came into the last room to finish our prayers, which happened to be the utility room, the older brother said, "Did you see that?"

When we assured him that we hadn't seen anything, he explained that he had seen a spirit exit the room through the outer wall. I happened to be facing him at the time, so I did not see what he had seen.

We continued in our praying and asked God to station angels in her home and at the property lines. The home was now cleansed.

A year later, I stopped by to ask how things were going. She told me things were good. In fact, she told me that no more problems had occurred, and the peace of God now reigned in her home.

The following is a sample prayer that you may adapt and use in praying for your home. Allow me to use it to pray for your home:

Dear Father God,

I bring before You the home of this reader. Whether it is a house, an apartment, a rented room, or any other type of dwelling, I cover it with the blood of Jesus Christ. The very top of the structure, the outside, and everything inside is covered. Lord, I pray that Jesus' blood would go down to the foundation and out to the property lines. Please forgive any sins that have taken place in this home or have taken place upon the ground where this dwelling was built. I am sorry for the pain these sins have caused You; please forgive them.

Father, please station Your angels in this dwelling and at the corners of the property lines right now. If there should be any demons in the home or residing on this property, please instruct Your angels to escort them away right now and send them wherever You tell them to go.

Father, please release Your Presence and live with those who call this place home in unity and peace. May Your love fill their home now in the name of Jesus Christ, amen.

6

For Ministries

I want to thank all the ministers who are working for the Lord in furthering His kingdom. I am saddened by statistics that indicate some fifteen hundred pastors leave the pastorate each month here in America. Many of these men and women of God suffer from burnout and must attend to other needs. My path also often crosses with many pastors who work a full-time job in addition to serving as the senior pastor of a church.

On January 1, 2011, the Lord gave me a vision. The message was dire—one that I would rather not share but know that I must. America has lost its hedge of protection from evil influences. I saw second-level demons rushing into America, and their first attack was launched at the churches across the nation. On the same day in the following year, I witnessed another similar vision. This time the third-

and fourth-level demons were ready to attack believers.

I believe God's people are now undergoing spiritual attacks on levels never before experienced.

I believe God's people are now undergoing spiritual attacks on levels never before experienced. In retrospect, I do not believe the church is ready for this type of spiritual warfare. Some believers want to conduct spiritual warfare head-on. I believe God has given believers a hedge of protection that we can apply to our lives. In the last few years, I have learned that living 2 Chronicles 7:14 will not only bring the individual believer a hedge of protection, but it will also change any ministry, period.

> *If my people, who are called by my name, will humble themselves and pray and seek my face and turn from their wicked ways [sins], then I will hear from heaven, and I will forgive their sin and will heal their land* (2 Chronicles 7:14).

Apply this Scripture to your ministry because God is releasing an inheritance to the church, and those who have a childlike heart will gain His presence.

Some people in our country are throwing the doors wide open to the occult.

I want to encourage all pastors to read *Needless Casualties of War* by John Paul Jackson. This book will open your eyes and change your approach in seeking God's protection from the evil one. In addition, some people in our country are throwing the doors wide open to the occult. Most of them are simply dabbling in the darkness; however, some of them have tapped into serious dark powers, and they are inflicting harm upon the church.

For this reason, I developed the following prayer for ministries. I have learned how spiritual doors are forced open by evil, and this prayer is designed to close those doors and to bring angelic protection to Christian lives and ministries. Let's pray the following prayer together.

Dear Father God,

Please cover this ministry with the blood of Christ from the very top of the structure to the bottom—down to the foundation and out to the property lines. Please cover everything outward and everything inward in the blood. Please wash it as clean and as white as snow.

Father, please station Your angels inside the building and outside on the corners of the property. If a high-ranking angel is needed to protect this ministry, please assign that angel to that position now. Father, if any sins have taken place in this building and upon the ground on which it sits, we are sorry for these sins. We are sorry for the pain these sins have caused You. Please forgive them.

For all ministries in which corporate sin has taken place, I ask that You would please forgive these sins and release unity. Also, Lord, if there should be any curses, spells, voodoo, or occult activities sent toward this ministry and the staff, we break them off and cast them away right now in the name of Jesus. Should there be any demons in the building or on the ground, please instruct Your angels to escort them away and send them wherever You tell them to go.

We anoint this structure with Your holy oil and set it apart for Your work. Would You please release Your presence into this ministry? Father, please make it an intersection of heaven and earth where people can come and experience Your presence. I ask, Lord, that Your daughter—the church and the ministry—would inherit the land and all Your provisions to enrich it and protect it. May an abundant harvest take place as You remove all the hindrances holding back the ebbing flow of Your grace to become a deluge without limits.

Please let revival come to this church and ministry as You have for this new

day in these final days. Lord, if any spe-
cific sins need to be repented of, reveal
them to Your people that they will be
forgiven. In Jesus' name, amen.

Pastor Phillip Corbett has written a book, entitled
Running With Your Second Wind, to help pastors
attract the presence of God. You can see more information about it at the back of this book.

7

Vows and Word Curses

Our spoken words have life. They can set our life on a path we did not intend to take, or they can keep our life on the right path.

At times we casually say, "I will never love again," or, "No one will ever hurt me again." At some point in your life, someone might have told you that you will never amount to anything.

These examples of vows and word curses need to be broken over our lives. Spend some time asking God to show you if you have released any vows. Make a comprehensive list. Also, make a list of things you have heard other people say about you. Have they limited your growth? Have you allowed these vows and word curses to remain active in your life?

Long ago, in a mere instant, my father said some condescending remarks about me. Those words planted a seed that grew. It is simply that easy to happen in life.

The following two prayers are designed to help a person dealing with vows and word curses.

Dear Father,

If the people praying this prayer have made any vows or ungodly declarations, please bring them to mind. We renounce those vows in the name of Jesus Christ and end them right now— no longer giving them power. In the name of Jesus, we now release godly provision to replace those vows and invite Your Holy Spirit to come into those places and restore these people to godly health. In Jesus' name, amen.

And let's pray the following prayer regarding word curses:

Dear Father,

I know You have plans for my life. I want to experience the fullness of Your plans. I bring before You all the negative things people have said over me.

They were untrue then, and I do not want them to be a part of my life any longer. (Read from the list you made.) Father, in Jesus' name, please end all these word curses now and replace them with Your love and affirmation. Let me see Your potential for my life. Let me rest in the knowledge and peace that You alone have my best interests at heart. In Jesus' name, amen.

8

Open Heaven

This book has addressed the need to close bad spiritual doors. I also desire that God would open His wonderful spiritual doors in your life.

I consider myself an experiential Christian, which means I experience the Trinity often. In the same way, I want you to also experience the Lord in some wonderful ways in these last days. In the book of Joel, the Word of God says:

> *And afterward, I will pour out my Spirit on all people. Your sons and daughters will prophesy, your old men will dream dreams, your young men will see visions* (Joel 2:28).

Right before us is a wonderful outpouring of the Holy Spirit. In dreams, I have seen a tsunami-like wave of the Holy Spirit engulf His children. My desire for you is that the Holy Spirit will overtake you with wonderful blessings—like those that happened in the Upper Room on the day of Pentecost.

I have received reports from people who have read my book, *Healing the Nation.* After reading it, a missionary to Mexico said, "My heart is on fire for God." He added, "I began to see miracles happen when I ministered!"

My prayer is to see every one of my readers tap into God in a tangible way. My hope is that you would become a tool in the hands of God to work for Him in order to significantly impact His kingdom.

My hope is that you would become a tool in the hands of God to work for Him in order to significantly impact His kingdom.

The following are the words I heard for the few moments when I was experiencing my second heart attack and was dead. Instantly, I was in the spiritual realm, where Father God spoke to me and said that it is "only while you are on earth that you can work for

Jesus." These few words greatly impacted my life. I love to do the work of God. Living in the supernatural has been wonderful. Seeing lives changed because the Holy Spirit has interacted with one of His children brings great joy to my heart. Therefore, let's pray and expect God to do great things in your life.

Dear Father,

I lift up to You all Your children who read this prayer. Please open a window to heaven over their lives. Please pour out Your blessings without measure. Fill their hearts with Your love. Lord, please fill them with Your Holy Spirit and release the elements of Your Holy Spirit into their lives. May You give them Your living water to flow into their lives and refresh their spirits. May that living water well up within them and flow out to all their loved ones. Share with Your children, Lord, the wind of Your Holy Spirit and bring Your changes into their lives.

Place Your children's feet upon a path of Your design. Please release the power of Your Holy Spirit into them to create new things as only You can do. May Your new life and gifts bring change, direction, and blessing to Your children as well as their households.

Father, may the fire of Your passion burn within Your children's hearts and be contagious to all those who surround them. Lord, please allow Your anointed oil to flow upon Your children's heads. Let Your children be so related to the Holy Spirit, that You will open a life of works and ministry for them.

Father, please place Your favor upon Your children. May Your favor go before them in all parts of their lives and be a wonderful blessing. In Jesus' name we pray, amen.

As I minister to people online through a Christian ministry, I often ask, "Did you sense the presence of the Holy Spirit with you as you prayed these prayers?" Now I am asking you, my friend, the same question.

Did you likewise feel His presence? If so, please e-mail me at the following address and tell me all about it.

Healingthenation1776 @gmail.com.

May I also make another suggestion? This very night, invite the Holy Spirit to visit you and expect Him to show up. Don't limit Him to the night. Invite Him to visit you during the day as well.

One person who received the prayer for breaking generational sins was visiting the US from Africa. The day after the prayer, the Lord gave her a five-part vision of all the spiritual hindrances she was experiencing. We prayed together to break those points of bondage, and she began a new life in Jesus. Two weeks later, she returned to Africa with a new heart for God.

It is my hope that you will be on fire for God so that you can enjoy all the fullness of His kingdom!

I have written this booklet to pinpoint the prayers that can cleanse the spiritual atmosphere of your life, home, and ministry. These prayers have been taken from my book *Healing the Nation.* I also share many other stories and truths in that book. For instance, I describe the new move of God being released in Texas. I also share how God showed me that the Constitution of the United States is at risk and will fall. Quite simply, if we do not gain Father God's ear to turn and to reverse our spiritual downward spiral, we will not see an upward direction again. America, as we have known this nation, will come to an end.

It is my hope that you will experience the Holy Spirit and be Spirit-filled and on fire for God so that you can enjoy all the fullness of His kingdom!

9

Maintenance

After celebrating on Thanksgiving Day of 2010, we were cleaning up in the evening, and I passed by a darkened hallway. Because the hallway was dark, I saw a glowing ball of light about the size of a soccer ball about five feet above the floor. I stopped, turned, and started up the stairs to confront this intruder. As I approached, the light started moving away from me and entered the computer room. By the time I got up there, it was gone.

What did I learn from this confrontation? Quite simply, not everything left my home with our guests who had been visiting. At the same time, I believe that, through this experience, God allowed me to learn a lesson.

Because of this experience, I began to change my bedtime prayers. I realized that sometimes spiritual housecleaning touchups need to be done because of the spiritual doors that are always being opened and closed by our choice of activities. Connecting with other people allows spiritual activity. Other spiritual doors in your home include the television, the telephone, and the computer, to list a few. We all want godly connections in our lives; we all want to keep the evil influences out of our homes.

When we are sleeping, we are likewise vulnerable to the spiritual realm. We want God to interact with us in our dreams and give us visions. However, many people suffer from nightmares. Closing spiritual doors in our lives and homes helps us get a good night's sleep. However, other family members' activities affect everyone in the home. Each one must make an effort to live a holy life. I realize this may not be possible. But I'm thankful that God still provides a way for us to be spiritually protected. Pray and cover your bedroom to improve its spiritual atmosphere.

You need to develop nighttime prayers for your life. I start my prayers by saying,

Dear Father, if there are any evil spirits in the house or on the property, please have Your angels escort them away right now.

I then continue with,

Please tie and cut all cords to any ungodly people with whom I have connected today.

Next, I address spiritual doors.

Father, please close all spiritual doors in this house, including the television, the telephone, and the Internet. Close them off the property.

(You will need to discover your entry points.) I finish my prayer by asking that any vulnerable spots be closed as well. From these suggestions, you can easily construct your own prayer.

The Lord set my feet on a path
I never would have chosen.

The Lord set my feet on a path I never would have chosen. I have learned the spiritual tools needed to protect my life and my home. What you have read in these pages has taken the better part of twenty years of experience. Application is empowered by your faith in God. You must believe He is there for you. I want you to experience God, hear His voice, and learn to follow Him wherever He may lead you.

As a volunteer for a Christian ministry, I chat online with people who are suffering because their homes and their lives are wide open to the enemy. We need God to heal this land, especially the very land on which our homes are located, and our communities. We desperately need God to heal our nation. I truly believe that, if the Christian community would live 2 Chronicles 7:14, America would be changed.

> *If my people, who are called by my name, will humble themselves and pray and seek my face and turn from their wicked ways, then I will hear from heaven, and I will forgive their sin and will heal their land* (2 Chronicles 7:14).

God bless,

Tom Donnan

About the Author

Tom Donnan was pronounced clinically dead of a heart attack in February 2006. But God wasn't done with him. He brought Tom back to the land of the living with a burden to see revival come to America.

He frequently travels and ministers with Pastor Phillip Corbett. He has also written a book entitled *Healing the Nation*. He's married to Mary, his wife of 13 years, and has three grandchildren.

Contact Information

You can email Tom at:
Healingthenation1776@gmail.com

Other books you might like:

Healing the Nation
Tom Donnan
With a piercing word from God in his heart, Tom brings a dynamic vision of a new move of God to the church. He shares how each believer is designed to be a vital part of it, moving through repentance to a powerful walk in Christ.
ISBN 978158169-4734 $15.99 PB

Running With Your Second Wind
Phillip Corbett
We are in need of true revival and not just another series of meetings. For the pastor who hungers for a move of God...for the people who know there's something missing in their lives...this book will bring them to God's presence, and they will never be the same!
ISBN 978158169-4727 $14.99 PB

The Second Story Window
Phillip Corbett
Many people have been traumatized by past events in their lives. When a resulting condition cannot be remedied through conventional medicine, counsel, or prayer, the situation must be looked at on a deeper, spiritual level. The good news is that deliverance and hope can truly be found.
ISBN 978158169-5885 $5.99 PB